Profiles of the Presidents

RONALD W. REAGAN

★ ★ ★

Profiles of the Presidents

RONALD W. REAGAN

by Jean Kinney Williams

Content Adviser: Marlene Smith-Baranzini, Former Editor, *California History Quarterly*
Reading Adviser: Dr. Linda D. Labbo, Department of Reading Education, College of Education, The University of Georgia

Compass Point Books ◆ Minneapolis, Minnesota

Compass Point Books
151 Good Counsel Drive
P.O. Box 669
Mankato, MN 56002-0669

Photographs ©: Courtesy Ronald Reagan Library, cover, 1, 7, 8, 9, 10, 12, 14, 19, 21, 25 (bottom), 33, 35, 37, 38, 39, 41, 43, 45 (top), 48, 54 (left), 55 (left), 57 (left), 58 (top left); Topham Picturepoint, 6, 32, 46; Hulton/Archive by Getty Images, 11, 15, 16, 26, 40, 45 (bottom), 54 (right), 58 (bottom left); Bettmann/Corbis, 13, 17, 18, 22, 23, 24, 27, 28, 29, 30, 36, 56; Wally McNamee/Corbis, 25 (top), 34, 42, 44; Corbis, 31; Courtesy Ronald Reagan Foundation, 50, 59 (left); Galen Rowell/Corbis, 55 (right); PhotoDisc, 57 (right); NASA (right); DigitalVision, 59 (right).

Editors: E. Russell Primm, Emily J. Dolbear, Melissa McDaniel, and Catherine Neitge
Photo Researchers: Image Select International and Svetlana Zhurkina
Photo Selector: Linda S. Koutris
Designer/Page Production: The Design Lab/Les Tranby
Cartographer: XNR Productions, Inc.

Library of Congress Cataloging-in-Publication Data
Williams, Jean Kinney.
    Ronald W. Reagan / by Jean Kinney Williams.
      v. cm.— (Profiles of the presidents)
Includes bibliographical references (p.) and index.
Contents: A man of conviction—From Middle America—From "B" movies to writing his own scripts—In the White House—Building relations with the Soviet Union, rebounding from scandal—After the White House—Glossary—Ronald W. Reagan's life at a glance—Ronald W. Reagan's life and times—World events—Understanding Ronald W. Reagan and his presidency.
    ISBN 978-0-7565-0284-3 (hardcover)
    1. Reagan, Ronald—Juvenile literature. 2. Presidents—United States—Biography—Juvenile literature. [1. Reagan, Ronald. 2. Presidents.] I. Title. II. Series.
    E877 .W54 2003
    973.927'092—dc21   2002010046

Visit Compass Point Books on the Internet at *www.compasspointbooks.com*
or e-mail your request to *custserv@compasspointbooks.com*

RONALD W. REAGAN

Table of Contents

★   ★   ★

*NOTE: In this book, words that are defined in the glossary are
in **bold** the first time they appear in the text.*

The Great Communicator

★ ★ ★

When Ronald Reagan became president of the United States in 1981, the nation was facing a number of problems. Prices were rising quickly. Many people were without jobs. By the time Reagan left office in 1989, the U.S. economy was humming. More people had jobs,

Ronald Reagan ▶ served as president from 1981 to 1989.

and **inflation** was down. The U.S. military was the strongest in the world. The **cold war,** the long-standing tension between America and the Soviet Union, was close to its end.

Though Reagan had a longtime interest in politics, he became a politician late in life. He was fifty-five and had no government experience when he ran for governor of California in 1966. What he did have was a gift for explaining his strong, simple beliefs. California voters responded by electing him. Then, in 1980, voters all across America heard his message about patriotism, family, and lower taxes. The man known as the Great Communicator became the nation's fortieth president.

As president, Ronald Reagan was much admired, even by many of his critics. They liked his sincere beliefs. As his friend and close adviser George Shultz once said, "What you saw was what you got. And what you saw was really good, and very American."

◀ *Ronald Reagan (left) being sworn in as America's fortieth president*

From Middle America

★ ★ ★

Ronald Wilson Reagan was born on February 6, 1911, in Tampico, Illinois. He was the second of Jack and Nelle Reagan's two sons. Jack Reagan was a shoe salesman with a good sense of humor. Nelle Reagan was a gentle, nurturing woman and a devout Christian. The Reagans had little money. Nelle always had high hopes, however, and she often acted on her Christian principles by helping others who were more in need.

◄ Ronald Reagan (second from right) with his brother Neil and their parents in 1914

8

Reagan considered his childhood happy, although it had its painful moments. His father was an alcoholic. Reagan remembers coming home one winter day to find his father passed out, drunk, on the front steps. Eleven-year-old Ronald had to carry his father to bed. Like his mother, Reagan could push away such bad experiences with his hope and faith in the future.

▼ By the time he was ready to attend high school, Ronald lived in Dixon, Illinois.

During Ronald's childhood, the family moved from town to town in Illinois. They finally settled in Dixon, where Ronald and his older brother, Neil, went to high school.

Ronald was shy in high school. His friendliness and sense of humor, however, made him popular. His great memory also helped him out in the classroom.

Reagan earned money for his college tuition by working as a lifeguard.

Reagan's eyesight was so poor that he could not play sports such as baseball. He played on the football team, however, and became a good swimmer. He saved money to go to college by working as a lifeguard during the summers.

After high school, Reagan attended nearby Eureka College. During college, there were already hints of where his career would lead him. He won an award for his performance in a college play. He also became involved in student politics.

Reagan got his interest in politics from his father, who taught him to admire President Franklin Delano Roosevelt. The president guided Americans through much of the Great Depression, the severe economic crisis of the 1930s. During the Great Depression, millions of people lost their jobs and many lost their homes or suffered other hardships. Roosevelt was a **liberal** Democrat. He believed that it was the government's duty to help

people. So he created many government programs to help Americans who were poor and jobless because of the depression. He was the first president Ronald Reagan voted for. Reagan especially admired Roosevelt's "fireside chats," inspiring talks that were broadcast over the radio.

Reagan graduated from college in 1932 during the worst part of the depression. Jobs of any kind were scarce. He decided to look for work in radio.

◄ *President Roosevelt's "fireside chats" raised the spirits of Americans.*

Reagan was hired by station WOC in Davenport, Iowa, to announce college football games for $5 per afternoon. His casual, witty personality worked well on radio. He soon moved to WHO in Des Moines, Iowa. One of his duties was "covering" Chicago Cubs baseball games without ever leaving Des Moines. He read reports of the game as it occurred and then gave play-by-play on the radio, making it sound like he was actually at the game. His much-improved salary of $75 per week helped support his family.

One of Reagan's ◄ first jobs after college was working as an announcer for WHO Radio in Des Moines.

Reagan became a major radio personality in the Midwest. He soon turned his eye toward Hollywood. He

was in California covering baseball spring training in 1937 when an actress from Des Moines introduced him to her agent. The agent arranged a screen test, and Ronald Reagan signed a contract with Warner Brothers studios. A new chapter was beginning in Reagan's life.

To Hollywood and Beyond

★   ★   ★

Young Ronald Reagan was a handsome man, but he never became a major Hollywood star. Still, he carved out a good career playing nice guys like himself. Between 1937 and 1964, Reagan appeared in fifty-four movies. Only a few of them were memorable. Most of them were B movies—low-budget, predictable films that people watched but without high expectations.

▼ *Ronald Reagan married actress Jane Wyman in 1940.*

One of his more important early pictures was *Brother Rat*, which was released in 1938. His costar in that film was actress Jane Wyman. The two fell in love and were married in 1940. Their daughter, Maureen, was born in 1941.

By the early 1940s, Reagan's film career was improving as he won roles in bigger films such as *King's Row* and *Santa Fe Trail.* In *Knute Rockne–All American,* he portrayed George Gipp, who played football at the University of Notre Dame under the legendary coach Knute Rockne. In the film, Gipp is dying. On his deathbed he tells Rockne to "win one for the Gipper." "The Gipper" would later become one of Reagan's nicknames.

Reagan as "the ▼ *Gipper" in* Knute Rockne–All American

World War II (1939– 1945) interrupted Reagan's film career, and it never really recovered. When the United States entered the war in 1941, Reagan volunteered for the cavalry, an army unit that rides horses. He was refused, however, because of his poor eyesight. Instead, he was assigned to make training and promotional films for the army.

At this point in his life, Reagan was still a liberal Democrat. He was starting to have ideas, however, that would eventually lead him in other directions. During World War II, the United States fought on the same side as the Soviet Union. It had been formed in 1922 when Russia and other nations in Eastern Europe and Central Asia combined into one country. The Soviet Union practiced communism, meaning that the government owned all businesses and controlled the economy. Some Soviet leaders had people who disagreed with them arrested or even killed.

▲ The bombing of Pearl Harbor on December 7, 1941

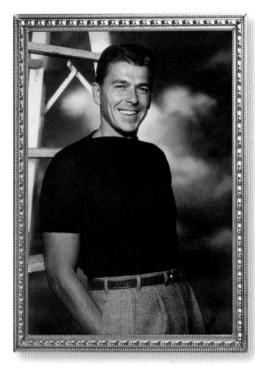

Although his acting career was never the same after the war, Reagan became president of the Screen Actors Guild in 1947.

By the time World War II ended in 1945, Reagan was wary of the Soviet Union. He had joined an organization made up of actor war veterans. He left the group when it refused to condemn Soviet policies.

Reagan was still very interested in politics. He often worked to help elect Democratic candidates. In 1947, he also became president of the Screen Actors Guild, the **union** that represents actors. As president of the union, he tried to work out agreements between the studios and the actors.

By this time, Reagan was more and more unhappy with the way his own career was going. He wasn't getting good roles. Warner Brothers "decided I wasn't a very big drawing card, and are afraid to risk giving me good parts," wrote Reagan to a friend at the time. Meanwhile, Jane Wyman's career was blossoming. She was nominated for an

Academy Award in 1947 for her role in *The Yearling.* Two years later she won the award for her role in *Johnny Belinda.* Although she and Reagan had adopted a son, Michael, who was born in 1945, they divorced in 1948. She blamed Reagan's ever increasing political activities.

⬩ *Jane Wyman (second from right) with other Academy Award winners in 1949*

Reagan left Warner Brothers for Universal Studios, but this didn't improve his status as an actor. In one movie, *Bedtime for Bonzo,* his costar was a chimpanzee.

Perhaps his film career lagged because it wasn't his true passion. Instead, his passion seemed to be his strong beliefs in opposing communism. He acted on these beliefs whenever he had the chance. In 1946, he had helped stop a **strike** by another actors' union, the Conference of Studio Unions, because it showed some support for communism. The next year, he went before a congressional **committee** that was investigating communism in Hollywood. He told them the names of people he believed were **communists**.

Reagan told a ▸ congressional committee the names of supposed communists in Hollywood.

Reagan had more chances to express his views when General Electric (GE) hired him to host a television series called "General Electric Theater." The job also required him to travel to GE plants and offices around the country. He could speak to company employees about whatever he wanted to, as long as he promoted GE products. This job gave Reagan the chance to perfect his public speaking skills. He learned to poke fun at himself while talking politics.

▾ *Reagan as the host of "General Electric Theater"*

The job also caused him to change his mind about the business world. When working for Democratic candidates in California, Reagan had sometimes complained that the Republicans supported "big business." He said that businesses' ever-higher profits came at the expense of low-paid workers. In traveling for GE, however, Reagan met businesspeople who reminded him of himself. Like Reagan, they had become wealthy by working hard. Reagan's political makeover was almost complete.

The Governor

★ ★ ★

With his casual style and good humor, Reagan became a popular speaker at banquets and business meetings. The more businesspeople he met, the more convinced he became that "big business" wasn't the problem. Instead, he was beginning to believe that "big government" was the problem. He thought that taxes were too high and that government imposed too many rules on businesses. Reagan had become a **conservative.**

Reagan's second wife, Nancy, was a partner in Reagan's changing politics. Reagan had met Nancy Davis in the late 1940s, when she was a young actress. She came from a family of wealthy Republicans who loved to talk politics. That interest in politics was something she and Reagan had in common. They were married in 1952. After she and Reagan starred together in a 1957 movie, *Hellcats of the Navy,* Nancy gave up acting to stay home with their two children, Patti and Ron.

In 1959, Reagan was again elected president of the Screen Actors Guild. He spoke out against communism while leading actors in a successful strike against the studios in 1959. Though still officially a Democrat, he acted more like a Republican in the voting booth. He was becoming a spokesman for conservative causes, as well.

In 1960, Reagan campaigned for Republican presidential candidate

▲ *Ronald and Nancy Reagan at their wedding*

Richard Nixon, who lost in a very close election to Democrat John F. Kennedy. In 1962, Reagan officially switched parties, becoming a Republican. That same year, "General Electric Theater" was canceled on television. Reagan began hosting another show called "Death Valley Days," but his acting career was coming to an end.

The Republican candidate for president in 1964 was Barry Goldwater, a conservative senator from Arizona. Goldwater's campaign was going poorly. Even many Republicans considered his views too extreme. Reagan was asked to give a speech for Goldwater at the Republican **convention.**

Reagan's speech was broadcast on national television. In it, he said that America could reach its full potential only if it reduced taxes and made government smaller. He also said that the United States had to stand up to the threat of

Many Americans believed Barry Goldwater's views were too extreme.

communism or risk "a thousand years of darkness." Reagan's speech was as conservative as anything Goldwater might have said. Yet Reagan came across as inspiring, rather than threatening. Goldwater lost the election, but Reagan captured the attention of California Republicans. They needed a candidate to run for governor in 1966.

Reagan faced the Democratic governor Edmund G. "Pat" Brown in the election. Brown considered Reagan a lightweight—just an actor with no political experience. Reagan painted his inexperience as an advantage: "I am an ordinary citizen with a deep-seated belief that much of what troubles us has been brought about by politicians."

◀ Reagan (second from left) admitted he had less experience than Brown, but he convinced voters that was to their advantage.

Ronald and Nancy
Reagan after
voting in 1966

He complained about high state taxes and about state budgets that weren't balanced. He also promised, if elected, to enforce law and order. Reagan came across as hopeful and having a sense of humor. He won the election by almost one million votes.

Most historians think Reagan was just an average governor. He actually increased some taxes. He didn't shrink the size of the state government as he had vowed during his campaign, but he kept the budget from growing. For example, to save money, he made changes in the state's welfare system, which helps needy people. As governor,

Reagan learned that sometimes giving in a little, or compromising, got his plans turned into law. This lesson would serve him well as president.

In 1968, he announced that he was running for president. Republicans instead chose former vice president Richard Nixon to be their candidate. Reagan returned to the governor's office. He was reelected in 1970.

When his second term as governor ended, Reagan bought a ranch in Santa Barbara, California. He wrote a newspaper column and made speeches. He also rode horses, chopped wood, and cleared brush on his ranch. He looked to 1976 as his year to run for the White House.

◄ Republicans chose Richard Nixon as their presidential candidate in 1968.

◄ Reagan at his Santa Barbara ranch

Jimmy Carter ▶

Reagan challenged President Gerald Ford to be the Republican candidate that year. Reagan campaigned hard. He said Ford had been too soft in dealing with the Soviet Union and China, another communist nation. Reagan only narrowly lost the Republican nomination to Ford. Ford then lost to the Democratic candidate, former Georgia governor Jimmy Carter.

Reagan's turn would come in 1980. By then, he was the top Republican in the nation. He easily became the Republican candidate for president. Reagan selected George H. W. Bush, a former diplomat and congressman from Texas, as his running mate for vice president.

President Jimmy Carter had been in office for one term. He proved to be an easy target for Reagan. Inflation, which had hurt Gerald Ford in the election four years earlier, was still a problem. Many people were without jobs. Carter's image as president was further damaged in 1979, when a group of angry Iranians stormed the U.S. **embassy** in Tehran, Iran's capital, and took fifty-three Americans hostage. The Americans were held hostage for more than a year, while the presidential election was being waged back in the United States. People expected President Carter to find a way to get the Americans home safely. When he took too long, they turned toward Reagan, hoping he would do something. The hostage crisis became a major issue in the election.

◄ *Iranians took over the U.S. embassy in their homeland and took Americans hostage.*

During a televised debate with the president, Reagan (right) convinced Americans they had not progressed very far under Carter's leadership.

In a televised debate between Reagan and Carter, Reagan asked viewers: "Are you better off now than you were four years ago?" With inflation at 12 percent and eight million people without jobs, a lot of Americans answered that question by voting for Ronald Reagan. Reagan received 51 percent of the votes to Carter's 42 percent. Independent candidate John Anderson got 7 percent. As Carter had before him, Reagan swept a sitting president from office.

In the White House

★   ★   ★

Just hours after he was sworn in as president, Ronald Reagan was able to give Americans some good news: The American hostages in Iran had been freed. The Iranian captors had waited for Reagan to take office to further embarrass former President Jimmy Carter.

▾ *The hostages in Iran were set free the day Reagan was sworn in as president.*

One of Reagan's first goals as president was to overhaul the federal budget. Right away, he proposed a combination of tax cuts and spending cuts. Reagan believed that if people and businesses paid fewer taxes, they would

spend that money on something else. By buying more products and services, they would create more jobs. The press nicknamed this economic theory "Reaganomics."

Reagan proposed cutting the budgets for many federal programs, including those for welfare, the arts, national parks, and the environment. Congress didn't approve all of the cuts Reagan wanted in 1981. Yet Congress did agree to decrease spending by $39 billion. They agreed to cut taxes, too.

While cutting costs in some areas, Reagan was committed to spending more money on the military. When

Reagan worked with Labor Secretary George Schultz to try to create more jobs.

Reagan arrived in Washington, D.C., in 1981, the cold war was still on. The United States and the Soviet Union did not trust each other. So Reagan asked Congress for an additional $180 billion for the armed forces.

Reagan had big plans for the military. He wanted to put nuclear missiles in Europe to keep the Soviets at bay. He also announced plans for a space-based defense system, the Strategic Defense Initiative (SDI). Reporters nicknamed it "Star Wars." The theory was that weapons in space would be able to shoot any Soviet missiles out of the air before they hit the United States.

◄ *Reagan announced his Strategic Defense Initiative during a television broadcast.*

Reagan was as opposed to communism as ever. In October 1983, he had a chance to act on these beliefs when communists took over the government of Grenada, a small island in the Caribbean Sea. The leaders of other Caribbean islands, such as Barbados and Jamaica, were concerned that communists might also take over their governments. They asked the United States for help. Reagan quickly decided to send troops to Grenada. The American military ousted the communists, and then American soldiers withdrew from the island.

A. U.S. helicopter ▶ on the island of Grenada

Reagan's military and economic plans drew plenty of fire from critics. In both the United States and Europe, there were huge protest rallies opposing his military buildup. His budget cuts were often criticized as shortsighted and damaging to the nation's quality of life. Facing such complaints, Reagan often showed two qualities for which he was known. The first was confidence that he was doing the right thing. The second was humor.

Reagan kept his sense of humor, even under the most difficult circumstances. On March 30, 1981, only two months into his presidency, he was shot and seri-

◀ Reagan was shot seconds after this photo was taken in front of the Washington Hilton Hotel in Washington, D.C.

ously injured by a mentally ill man named John Hinckley. Yet when his worried wife arrived at the hospital, Reagan downplayed his condition by cracking, "Honey, I forgot to duck." As doctors wheeled him into the operating room for surgery, he joked, "I hope you're all Republicans."

Many reporters were fond of the wisecracking president, even when they didn't agree with him. It was members of the press who nicknamed him "the Gipper." When Reagan recovered from his gunshot wound, he appeared before Congress and received a roaring round of applause. His budget, which so many members of Congress had criticized, was passed. His popularity with the public soared as well.

Speaker of the House ▶ Thomas "Tip" O'Neill (standing, right) and Vice President George Bush joined the rest of Congress in applauding Reagan during his first speech after the assassination attempt.

Reagan brought a relaxed style of leadership to the White House. It was so relaxed that he was sometimes accused of being lazy. He turned seventy as his first term began, and he always paced himself so he wouldn't get too worn out over the course of the day. He seldom arrived at his White House office before 9 A.M., and he rested at times during the day. He and Nancy often spent weekends at the presidential retreat, Camp David. They also took long vacations at their California ranch.

Reagan introduced the White House to a new and more relaxed method of leadership.

Reagan was sometimes involved in figuring out the details of a policy. More often, he gave that job to his aides and advisers. Secretary of Defense Caspar Weinberger was told to figure out how to beef up the military. A young Michigan congressman named David Stockman was put in charge of the Office of Management and Budget. His job was to hammer out Reagan's proposed budget cuts.

Reagan trusted advisers such as Caspar Weinberger to make certain policy decisions.

In 1984, Reagan ran for a second term. The Democrat running against him was Walter Mondale, who had been Jimmy Carter's vice president. Mondale chose Geraldine Ferraro, a congresswoman from New York, as his running mate. She was the first woman to appear on a major party's presidential ticket.

During the campaign, Mondale criticized how much Reagan's military buildup was putting the government into debt. Reagan just reminded voters that inflation was finally down. He won reelection easily.

▲ *Walter Mondale (right) said Reagan's military spending was costing the U.S. government too much money.*

Reagan returned to the White House as the oldest American president in history.

Ronald Reagan's ▶
official portrait
from his second
term as president

Trouble at Home and Abroad

★   ★   ★

In his second term, Reagan continued his efforts to shrink the federal government while expanding the military.

Reagan put money into researching SDI. In the meantime, he had a meeting with the new Soviet leader, Mikhail Gorbachev. Reagan was pleasantly surprised by Gorbachev. He called him "a different kind of Soviet leader." They met in Switzerland in 1985 and in Iceland the next year. Both

◀ Reagan met with Mikhail Gorbachev (right) to discuss reducing weapons in both the United States and the Soviet Union.

times they talked of reducing the number of weapons their countries had. In later years, Reagan recalled what he told Gorbachev during these meetings: "I'll tell you now, you can't win the arms race."

At home, Reagan asked Congress to rewrite the tax laws. He wanted them to create a simpler system.

In 1986, the United States faced a national tragedy. The space shuttle *Challenger* exploded soon after takeoff. Americans were shocked. Reagan, always aware of his role as the country's leader, went on television and movingly

The space shuttle ▶
Challenger
exploded soon
after takeoff
in 1986.

expressed his and the nation's grief over the accident.

Terrorism was a problem throughout the Reagan years. In Reagan's first term, a car bomb exploded at U.S. Marine barracks in the Middle Eastern country of Lebanon, killing 225 Americans. In June 1985, a U.S. jet was hijacked as it left Greece, and its passengers were kept hostage for seventeen days. Months later, an Italian cruise ship was hijacked, and an elderly American man was murdered. Then, in April 1986, a bomb went off in

▾ *The Reagans paying tribute to the victims of the bombing in Beirut*

a German nightclub. It killed two people, one of whom was an American soldier.

Libyan leader Muammar al-Qaddafi was thought to be involved in some of these events. Reagan ordered U.S. bombers to attack Qaddafi's military headquarters in Tripoli, the Libyan capital. Polls showed 70 percent of Americans approved of this response.

People weren't so happy with Reagan's response to a

Muammar al- ▶
Qaddafi

★

later terrorist event. Americans were kidnapped in Lebanon. The president's advisers believed Iranians were involved in the kidnappings. Reagan stated publicly that he would not bargain with terrorists to free the hostages, but he approved a secret deal to do just that. The United States agreed to sell weapons to Iran, which was at war with Iraq at the time, in exchange for the kidnapped Americans. This was illegal. After the Iranian hostage crisis of 1979, Congress had outlawed the selling of arms to Iran.

Meanwhile Reagan was unaware of the actions of

◀ *Reagan discussing the controversial sale of weapons to Iran*

National Security Adviser John Poindexter

Lieutenant Colonel Oliver North, an aide to National Security Adviser John Poindexter. North took money from the arms sale and gave it to the Contras in Nicaragua. The Contras were rebelling against the communist government in Nicaragua. Giving military aid to the Contras was also illegal. Congress had outlawed it in 1984.

Both the Reagan administration's secret deal with Iran and North's illegal aid to the Contras were revealed in 1986. These events became known as the Iran-Contra affair. Congress decided to investigate the matter. Suddenly, the president had a lot of explaining to do. He had to admit that he did not always know what his staff was doing. His public image took a beating.

That image got a boost in December 1987 when

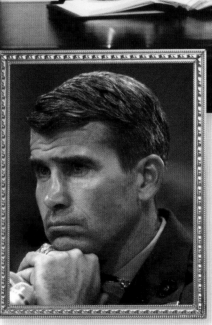

◀ *Reagan and Gorbachev signed a treaty in 1987 that marked the beginning of a better friendship between the United States and the Soviet Union.*

◀ *Lieutenant Colonel Oliver North*

Gorbachev came to Washington to sign an arms control treaty. The treaty reduced the number of missiles both the United States and the Soviet Union had. The treaty marked a welcome and major "thaw" in the decades-old cold war.

Ronald Reagan's eight years as president ended in

★

January 1989. Many people considered his presidency successful. When he left office, the stock market was strong and the cold war had eased. Americans elected George H. W. Bush the next president in part because he had served as Reagan's vice president.

The stock market ▼ was doing well by the end of Reagan's presidency.

Some aspects of Reagan's presidency were not so suc-

cessful. His military buildup left behind a large national debt. Reagan knew of this problem. He explained his policies by saying that when it came to choosing between the security of America and a large debt, "I'd have to come down on the side of national defense." That was sometimes an unpopular decision. By sticking

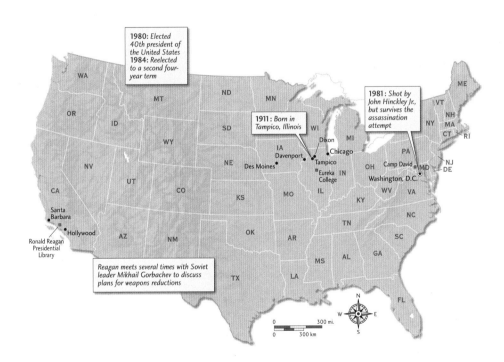

1980: Elected 40th president of the United States
1984: Reelected to a second four-year term

1911: Born in Tampico, Illinois

1981: Shot by John Hinckley Jr., but survives the assassination attempt

Ronald Reagan Presidential Library

Reagan meets several times with Soviet leader Mikhail Gorbachev to discuss plans for weapons reductions

to it, Reagan again showed confidence in his beliefs. Historian Paul Johnson has written that Reagan's self-assurance helped "restore the will and self-confidence of the American people."

Ronald and Nancy ▶
Reagan preparing to
leave Washington,
D.C., on his last
day in office

After the White House

★　★　★

After George H. W. Bush was sworn in as president in January 1989, Ronald and Nancy Reagan retired to California. Then, in 1994, Reagan announced he had Alzheimer's disease, which often strikes elderly people. The disease causes them to slowly lose their memory and their health. Reagan and his wife lived very privately until his June 5, 2004, death at his Bel-Air, California, home. He was ninety-three.

Reagan's daughter Patti Davis wrote a touching article about important lessons her father taught her as a girl on their ranch. In one horseback outing, Patti's horse was afraid to cross a shallow stream. She wanted to get off the horse and lead it through the water. "But my father wouldn't let me," Davis recalls. "Just stay on him and talk to him, and let him know what you want him to do," Reagan advised his daughter. After several minutes, Davis coaxed her horse to the other side of the stream where her father waited. "My father," she wrote, "considered fear a waste of time."

The first page of ▶ Reagan's letter to the nation announcing his Alzheimer's disease

GLOSSARY

★ ★ ★

cold war—the conflict between the United States and the USSR that did not result in actual war

committee—a group working together on a project

communists—followers of an economic system in which all businesses are owned by the government

conservative—believing that the government should have a limited role in people's lives

convention—a large meeting during which a political party chooses its candidates

embassy—a building in one country where the representatives of another country work

inflation—an economic state in which prices of goods and services continue to rise

liberal—believing that the government should help people in need by taking a larger role in their lives

strike—when workers refuse to work, hoping to force their company to agree to their demands

terrorism—the use of violence to make people or a nation do something

union—an organization of workers

RONALD W. REAGAN'S LIFE AT A GLANCE

★ ★ ★

PERSONAL

Nickname:	The Great Communicator, The Gipper, Dutch
Born:	February 6, 1911
Birthplace:	Tampico, Illinois
Father's name:	John Edward Reagan
Mother's name:	Nelle Wilson Reagan
Education:	Graduated from Eureka College in 1932
Wives' names:	Jane Wyman (1914–); Nancy Davis Reagan (1923–)
Married:	January 25, 1940, divorced 1948; March 4, 1952
Children:	Maureen Elizabeth Reagan (1941–2001); Michael Edward Reagan (1945–); Patricia Ann Reagan (1952–); Ronald Prescott Reagan (1958–)
Died:	June 5, 2004, in Bel-Air, California
Buried:	Ronald Reagan Presidential Library and Museum Simi Valley, California

PUBLIC

Occupation before presidency:	Actor, public official
Occupation after presidency:	Retired
Military service:	Served in the Army Air Force Motion Picture Unit, 1942–1945
Other government positions:	Governor of California
Political party:	Republican
Vice president:	George H. W. Bush
Dates in office:	January 20, 1981– January 20, 1989
Presidential opponents:	Jimmy Carter (Democrat) and John B. Anderson (Independent), 1980; Walter F. Mondale (Democrat), 1984
Number of votes (Electoral College):	43,267,489 of 83,820,086 (489 of 538), 1980; 53,428,357 of 90,359,280 (525 of 538), 1984
Selected Writings:	*Where's the Rest of Me?* (1965), *The Creative Society* (1968), *Abortion and the Conscience of the Nation* (1984), *Speaking My Mind* (1989), *An American Life* (1990)

★

Ronald Wilson Reagan's Cabinet

Secretary of state:
Alexander M. Haig Jr. (1981–1982)
George P. Shultz (1982–1989)

Secretary of the treasury:
Donald T. Regan (1981–1985)
James A. Baker III (1985–1988)
Nicholas F. Brady (1988–1989)

Secretary of defense:
Caspar W. Weinberger (1981–1987)
Frank C. Carlucci (1987–1989)

Attorney general:
William French Smith (1981–1985)
Edwin Meese (1985–1988)
Dick Thornburgh (1988–1989)

Secretary of the interior:
James G. Watt (1981–1983)
William P. Clark (1983–1985)
Donald P. Hodel (1985–1989)

Secretary of agriculture:
John R. Block (1981–1986)
Richard E. Lyng (1986–1989)

Secretary of commerce:
Malcolm Baldrige (1981–1987)
C. William Verity (1987–1989)

Secretary of labor:
Raymond J. Donovan (1981–1985)
William Brock (1985–1987)
Ann Dore McLaughlin (1987–1989)

Secretary of health and human services:
Richard S. Schweiker (1981–1983)
Margaret M. Heckler (1983–1985)
Otis R. Bowen (1985–1989)

Secretary of education:
Terrel H. Bell (1981–1985)
William J. Bennett (1985–1988)
Lauro F. Cavazos Jr. (1988–1989)

Secretary of housing and urban development:
Samuel R. Pierce Jr. (1981–1989)

Secretary of transportation:
Andrew L. Lewis Jr. (1981–1983)
Elizabeth H. Dole (1983–1987)
James H. Burnley (1987–1989)

Secretary of energy:
James B. Edwards (1981–1982)
Donald P. Hodel (1982–1985)
John Herrington (1985–1989)

RONALD W. REAGAN'S LIFE AND TIMES

★   ★   ★

REAGAN'S LIFE

WORLD EVENTS

February 6, Ronald Reagan is born in Tampico, Illinois — 1911

1913 — Henry Ford begins to use standard assembly lines to produce automobiles (below)

1920

Graduates from Dixon High School — 1928

1930 — 1930 — Designs for the first jet engine are submitted to the Patent Office in Britain

Graduates from Eureka College — 1932

1933 — Nazi leader Adolf Hitler is named chancellor of Germany

1935 — George Gershwin's *Porgy and Bess* opera opens in New York

Signs an acting contract with Warner Brothers — 1937

REAGAN'S LIFE

Stars in *Knute Rockne–All-American* — 1940

Marries Jane Wyman

Serves in Army Air Force Motion Picture Unit — 1942–1945

Becomes president of the Screen Actors Guild — 1947

Divorced from Jane Wyman — 1948

Marries Nancy Davis (below) — 1952

Again elected president of the Screen Actors Guild — 1959

1940

1950

WORLD EVENTS

1941   December 7, Japanese bombers attack Pearl Harbor, Hawaii, and America enters World War II

1942   Japanese Americans are placed in internment camps due to fear of disloyalty

1944   DNA (deoxyribonucleic acid) is found to be the basis of heredity

1945   America drops atomic bombs on the Japanese cities of Hiroshima and Nagasaki to end World War II

1953   The first Europeans climb Mount Everest (above)

1955   Disneyland, the first theme park in the United States, opens in Anaheim, California

1959   Fidel Castro becomes prime minister of Cuba

REAGAN'S LIFE   WORLD EVENTS

1960

1961   Soviet cosmonaut Yuri
        Gagarin is the first
        human to enter space

        The Berlin Wall is built,
        dividing East and West
        Germany

"GE Theater" canceled;   1962   1962-   Pope John XXIII calls
becomes host of   1965   the Second Vatican
"Death Valley Days"   Council, modernizing
on television   Roman Catholicism

                                      1963   Dr. Michael De Bakey
                                              first uses an artificial
                                              heart to take over a
                                              person's circulation
                                              during heart surgery

                                              Kenya becomes an
                                              independent republic

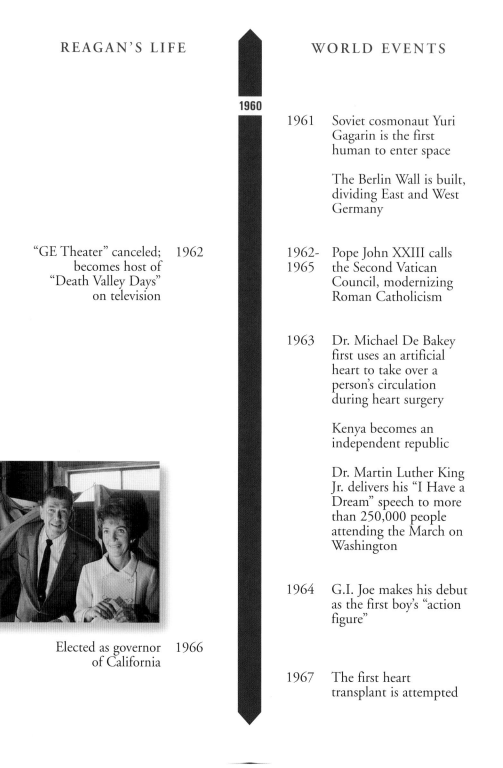

                                              Dr. Martin Luther King
                                              Jr. delivers his "I Have a
                                              Dream" speech to more
                                              than 250,000 people
                                              attending the March on
                                              Washington

                                      1964   G.I. Joe makes his debut
                                              as the first boy's "action
                                              figure"

Elected as governor   1966
of California

                                      1967   The first heart
                                              transplant is attempted

REAGAN'S LIFE

WORLD EVENTS

1970

1971   The 26th Amendment
to the Constitution is
ratified, allowing
18-year-olds to vote

Loses Republican   1976
presidential
nomination to
Gerald R. Ford

1978   The first test-tube baby
conceived outside its
mother's womb is born
in Oldham, England

1980

Presidential Election Results:		Popular Votes	Electoral Votes
1980	Ronald W. Reagan	*43,267,489*	*489*
	James E. Carter	*34,964,583*	*49*
1984	Ronald W. Reagan	*53,428,357*	*525*
	Walter F. Mondale	*36,930,923*	*13*

March, is shot by John   1981
W. Hinckley Jr.

August, Economic
Recovery Tax Act gives
the largest tax cut in
U.S. history

Appoints Sandra Day
O'Connor as the first
woman on the U.S.
Supreme Court

1982   Maya Lin designs the
Vietnam War Memorial
(below), commemorating
the Americans who died

REAGAN'S LIFE

The United States 1983
sends troops to
Grenada to oust
communists who have
taken power

October, terrorists blow
up a Marine barracks
in Beirut, Lebanon,
killing 225 soldiers

The Iran-Contra 1986
affair, involving
Oliver North (above),
becomes public

The United States and
the Soviet Union sign a
treaty to reduce
weapons

WORLD EVENTS

1983 The AIDS (acquired
immune deficiency
syndrome) virus is
identified

1986 The U.S. space shuttle
Challenger explodes
(above), killing all seven
astronauts on board

REAGAN'S LIFE			WORLD EVENTS
Publishes his autobiography, *An American Life*	1990	**1990** 1990	Political prisoner Nelson Mandela, a leader of the anti-apartheid movement in South Africa, is released; Mandela becomes president of South Africa in 1994
The Ronald Reagan Presidential Library opens in California	1991	1991	The Soviet Union collapses and is replaced by the Commonwealth of Independent States
			Conflict between Iraq and Kuwait in the Persian Gulf begins
Announces that he has Alzheimer's disease (below)	1994	1994	Genocide of 500,000 to 1 million of the minority Tutsi group by rival Hutu people in Rwanda
		2000 2000	Draft of the human genome is completed
		2001	Terrorist attacks on the two World Trade Center towers (right) in New York City and on the Pentagon near Washington, D.C., leave thousands dead
Dies June 5 at age ninety-three at his Bel-Air, California, home	2004	2004	Huge tsunami strikes nations bordering the Indian Ocean, killing tens of thousands of people and leaving many more homeless

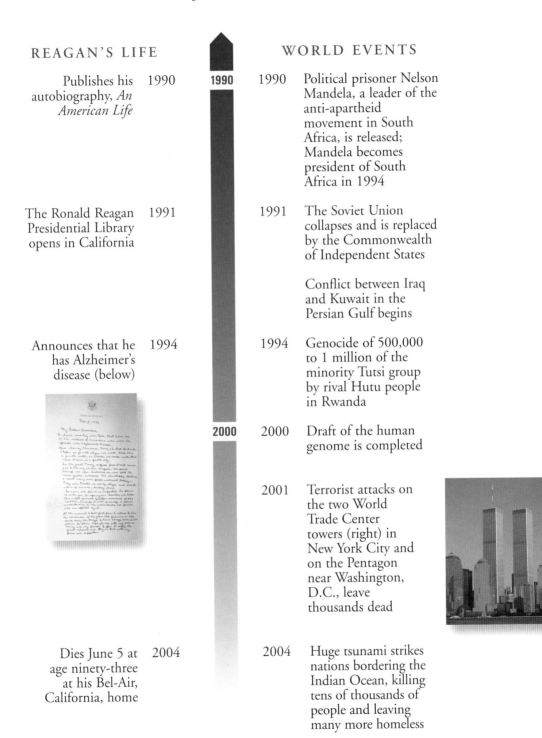

UNDERSTANDING RONALD W. REAGAN AND HIS PRESIDENCY

★　★　★

FURTHER READING

Dunham, Montrew, and Meryl Henderson. *Ronald Reagan: Young Leader.* New York: Aladdin, 1999.

Johnson, Darv. *The Reagan Years.* San Diego: Greenhaven Press, 1999.

Judson, Karen. *Ronald Reagan.* Springfield, N.J.: Enslow, 1997.

Orr, Tamra. *Ronald Reagan.* Philadelphia: Mason Crest Publishers, 2003.

ON THE WEB

For more information on this topic, use FactHound.

1. Go to *www.facthound.com*
2. Type in this book ID: 0756502845
3. Click on the *Fetch It* button.

FactHound will find the best Web sites for you.

REAGAN HISTORIC SITES
ACROSS THE COUNTRY

Ronald Reagan Birthplace
111 South Main Street
Tampico, IL 61283
815/438-2130
To see the apartment where
Reagan was born

**The Ronald Reagan
Presidential Foundation**
40 Presidential Drive
Simi Valley, CA 93065
805/522-2977
To visit a museum and library
dedicated to Reagan

THE U.S. PRESIDENTS
(Years in Office)

★ ★ ★

1. George Washington
   (March 4, 1789-March 3, 1797)
2. John Adams
   (March 4, 1797-March 3, 1801)
3. Thomas Jefferson
   (March 4, 1801-March 3, 1809)
4. James Madison
   (March 4, 1809-March 3, 1817)
5. James Monroe
   (March 4, 1817-March 3, 1825)
6. John Quincy Adams
   (March 4, 1825-March 3, 1829)
7. Andrew Jackson
   (March 4, 1829-March 3, 1837)
8. Martin Van Buren
   (March 4, 1837-March 3, 1841)
9. William Henry Harrison
   (March 6, 1841-April 4, 1841)
10. John Tyler
    (April 6, 1841-March 3, 1845)
11. James K. Polk
    (March 4, 1845-March 3, 1849)
12. Zachary Taylor
    (March 5, 1849-July 9, 1850)
13. Millard Fillmore
    (July 10, 1850-March 3, 1853)
14. Franklin Pierce
    (March 4, 1853-March 3, 1857)
15. James Buchanan
    (March 4, 1857-March 3, 1861)
16. Abraham Lincoln
    (March 4, 1861-April 15, 1865)
17. Andrew Johnson
    (April 15, 1865-March 3, 1869)

18. Ulysses S. Grant
    (March 4, 1869-March 3, 1877)
19. Rutherford B. Hayes
    (March 4, 1877-March 3, 1881)
20. James Garfield
    (March 4, 1881-Sept 19, 1881)
21. Chester Arthur
    (Sept 20, 1881-March 3, 1885)
22. Grover Cleveland
    (March 4, 1885-March 3, 1889)
23. Benjamin Harrison
    (March 4, 1889-March 3, 1893)
24. Grover Cleveland
    (March 4, 1893-March 3, 1897)
25. William McKinley
    (March 4, 1897-
    September 14, 1901)
26. Theodore Roosevelt
    (September 14, 1901-
    March 3, 1909)
27. William Howard Taft
    (March 4, 1909-March 3, 1913)
28. Woodrow Wilson
    (March 4, 1913-March 3, 1921)
29. Warren G. Harding
    (March 4, 1921-August 2, 1923)
30. Calvin Coolidge
    (August 3, 1923-March 3, 1929)
31. Herbert Hoover
    (March 4, 1929-March 3, 1933)
32. Franklin D. Roosevelt
    (March 4, 1933-April 12, 1945)

33. Harry S. Truman
    (April 12, 1945-
    January 20, 1953)
34. Dwight D. Eisenhower
    (January 20, 1953-
    January 20, 1961)
35. John F. Kennedy
    (January 20, 1961-
    November 22, 1963)
36. Lyndon B. Johnson
    (November 22, 1963-
    January 20, 1969)
37. Richard M. Nixon
    (January 20, 1969-
    August 9, 1974)
38. Gerald R. Ford
    (August 9, 1974-
    January 20, 1977)
39. James Earl Carter
    (January 20, 1977-
    January 20, 1981)
40. Ronald Reagan
    (January 20, 1981-
    January 20, 1989)
41. George H. W. Bush
    (January 20, 1989-
    January 20, 1993)
42. William Jefferson Clinton
    (January 20, 1993-
    January 20, 2001)
43. George W. Bush
    (January 20, 2001-)

INDEX

★ ★ ★

ABOUT THE AUTHOR

Jean Kinney Williams lives and writes in Cincinnati, Ohio. Her nonfiction books for children include biographies, a series of books about American religions, and several books about historical events.